JOURNEY WITH ME

A Collection of Poems by

Donald Cameron

A.H. STOCKWELL
PUBLISHERS SINCE 1898

Published in 2023 by
Donald Cameron
in association with
Arthur H Stockwell Ltd
West Wing Studios
Unit 166, The Mall
Luton, Bedfordshire
ahstockwell.co.uk

British Library Cataloguing-in-Publication Data
A catalogue record for this book is
available from the British Library.
ISBN: 9780722352267

To Mum and Dad

Contents

The Last Breeze 1

Silver 2

The Pot 3

Glow 4

Wee Bit Red 5

Into the Blue 6

The Call 7

Samaritan 8

A Hint of Grey 9

The Straight and Narrow 10

The Wanderers 11

Breathless 12

Unison 13

Skein 14

In the Great Hall 15

A Single Chap 16

Passengers 17

Loon 18

Ride On 19

Salvation 20

Sair 21

To the Last 22

Lucky Dip 23

This Way and That 24

The Nod 25

Allsorts 26

First Impression 27

The Big Brown 28

Dark 29

Recall 30

The Line 31

Trespass 32

The Depth of It 33
Time Stood Still 34
Hope 35
Phantom 36
Shadows 37
Lost 38
Above and Beyond 39
Here and There 40
Something In the Air 41
Edge 42
Still Here 43
Point of Origin 44
Speck 45
A Changing Landscape 46
The White Stuff 47
Ubiquitous 48
Blinkered 49
Embrace 50
H 51
Journey 52
Timeless 53
Who Gave Their All 54
Horizon 55
Behold 56
Cherish 57
One 58
In Appreciation of Ewe 59
Just the Two of Us 60
Dunking 61
The Awakening 62
The Cheek of It 63
A Change of Tack 64
Time Machine 65
A Final Note 66

JOURNEY WITH ME

The Last Breeze

To gaze upon this sunshine as day replaces night
And look to skies foreboding, with mischief in thy light
She strolls across the seven seas in all her shades of grey
From all four corners heaven-sent and just a touch of spray

Those that can take shelter as nature can but hide
Onward goes this mariner with faith on a morning tide
With rain to sting this weary face and chill the very soul
Clouds so stained with darkness, cruel waves that take their toll

A soft caress on a summer's day, like a kiss upon the brow
The golden fields roll gentle, dust gathers upon the plough
Chastised the mighty oak and beech, now robbed of limb and leaf
And stripped this land of colours so, her seasons all too brief

She laid the snow in winters hard and shook the rugged cross
To fan the flames on battlefields as carnage danced with loss
She treats them all as equals and sends them on their way
Time alone bears witness to all she had to say

Yet white-capped peaks hold steadfast, as far of seas do swell
Like old friends reacquainted, so much they have to tell
But now this morn so tranquil she turns and slips away
Like the passing of a loved one, oh to share just one more day

Silver

Wearied stone this path of old and steps we now do take
A faint sound so familiar, my soul it does awake
Where stubble fields lie silent, only moved by summer haze
Trees that live in shadows, stand quiet as if to gaze

How many have seen this silver and shared with me this day
I chance upon a single tern, white turns upon the grey
Who knelt here with their father and learnt her every mood
To understand her secrets like those before me could

This day so warm and gentle, the swifts unite to cheer
Fly high above the hidden depths for them no need of fear
Nature knows her every whim, the tides that come and go
What lies beneath is mystery, only seen by ebb and flow

Spate and drought a quick romance, the moon and stars do last
Each season a brief encounter, the same as in the past
A croy will turn attention, the bridge looks down in awe
The dam that tried appeasement, engulfed by an early thaw

Of all life's paths to follow, this one casts its spell
Times I see before me now, when all with life was well
As long as I am able and breath have I to roam
You'll find me beside my silver, the king of fish calls home

The Pot

As darkness throws its sullen cloak and light no more does wander
Pressed deep upon my every sense, this mind it stops to ponder
The woods that tempt me over, the burn that calls my name
Forgive this poor man's failing, to search for all things game

This land of colours before me, with daylight by my side
And see what passes by here, and where they often bide
For once I've learnt my quarry, and the moon does turn her back
I'll reach to wits about me, walk soft upon this track

With guardians all now bedded, no light or soul to see
Behold a constant presence, this fear that gnaws at me
The eyes can learn the darkness, every sound is friend and foe
With guile my close companion, this beating heart does go

The shadows watch my every move, the trees they seem to know
A stranger comes this way tonight, and tension starts to grow
No place this for the weary, be certain of all about
Stealth and hope edge forward, pray God I hear no shout

These woods so hushed and quiet, all who can stand still
Nature plays the waiting game, and time has she to fill
With the dawn upon its horizon, and the burn a raging deep
Fate sees me empty handed, till I meet a humble neep

Glow

Man and beast come calling, a fine pair dressed in black
Coal glints beneath the sunlight, proud horse in finest tack
Stood tall in all their glory, steam lifts to herald their strain
A hundredweight his penance, the man's face bears no pain

Driftwood hugs my shoulder, the windfall knows my axe
All in time for winter, with snow to fill all tracks
The shoreline delivers its bounty, but the wood hides all it can
Sweat and toil no stranger, in the seasons of a country man

These cold hands out before me, what hardship have they seen
Frozen outstretched fingers, every ounce of heat to glean
Such a glow restores all feeling, lifts spirits and that of joy
No better place come winter, for there sits man and boy

Strands of white curl upwards, a fleeting glance my way
The seasoned ash burns fiercely, for this its final day
All manner of shapes before me, with flames that gather pace
To capture my imagination, in the warmth of its embrace

Who rests before a winter's fire, the many and the meek
A mix of tales and laughter with a glow upon each cheek
The trusted axe lies dormant, the wood store dry and deep
And in the distance springtime, as fire gives way to sleep

Wee Bit Red

Amidst the quiet of winter's morn, as snowflakes drift my way
I lift a hand to feel their touch, their number who can say
Grey skies that promise plenty, as I gaze from east to west
And hear a song familiar, my friend so red of breast

I know not where he came from, I did not see him go
To hear this sweet recital, upon the sun-kissed snow
The summer is but mystery, our paths they never meet
This red so bright and vocal, to hedge and field of wheat

Perched bold upon the rowan tree, the master of all he sees
Behold the gaze from the darkest eye, to those in nearby trees
No time or quarter shall he give, for those who would but try
To venture forth in his domain, where titans clash and die

How cruel the winds of winter, driven snow and biting chill
To dance upon the open plain, lay waste to yonder hill
Yet here he sits resilient, through daylight and into dark
His silhouette a close companion, when all is bleak and stark

Winter in all its beauty, this land in finest white
Where hardship meets survival, the robin in all his might
Sat proud upon the holly bush, what lies in wait tomorrow
Come the spring he will depart, and leave a wee bit sorrow

Into the Blue

What brings me to these shallows, and beyond the blackest deep
Life balanced along the ledges, where mistakes bring endless sleep
Who knows this kind of freedom, and would dare to risk it all
They found me by the river, and I heard the pearler's call

Sat perched before the morning sun, yet not a word was spoke
A nod and glance sufficient, and then a well-rolled smoke
Fully clothed and into water, an ash stick by their side
We roamed into the unknown, and where the shells might bide

The current tugs on every move, my senses talk of cold
Body and soul seek compromise, as character starts to mould
Yet here I find acceptance, as the river meets my face
To focus on what lies beneath, and always a steady pace

I gaze upon the midday sun, and a warmth of total bliss
To illuminate this river bed, and her shells I nearly miss
Yet here I stand amidst the blue, like a poor man empty-handed
My fortune lies within the deep, pray God I don't get stranded

And see at last a muckle crook, alas we shall not meet
Sat so deep she almost smiles, as I begin to greet
I tell my tale around the fire, the spot where I had spied her
With shaking heads and words so wise, "Yer man's been on the cider"

The Call

Kings and Queens anointed, have felt it in their time
To have knelt in such a shadow, and them in firing line
Has touched the lowly commoner, and those in highest power
To such in darkest poverty, and nobles upon the tower

The man who's bound for gallows, and him that so declared
Colour and creed no saviour, there's none that shall be spared
From the Christian and the Samaritan, to the savage and the beast
To those of highest intellect, and them that ken the least

Some will walk as others run, and here's to them that's late
You cannot see it in the stars, but sure enough 'tis fate
To ponder on such dilemma, whilst others sit and dwell
The final seconds are but silence, 'tis heaven sent or hell

No words then upon the hour, for such a deed as this
Some might even close their eyes, in hope of total bliss
So here I squat upon this spot, no offering or token
And answer the call of nature, held close my only doken

Samaritan

Who comes when help is needed, no pause for second thought
A friend to all and sundry, for age does matter not
To hold my hand so tightly, this strength I know and trust
Such resilience in all weathers, its presence is a must

No words of praise are needed, and none have you to say
But time and again I need you, at night or in the day
At every time of asking, you ease my every load
So much that you can handle, upon life's weary road

And yet we are but strangers, and you without a name
Your silence is a constant, I hold you all the same
No prejudice or favourites, not one to discriminate
Transparent to the very last, and never are you late

What lies in store tomorrow, how many more like you
The isles we have travelled, and you appear brand new
But a gust of wind and parted, my heart can only sag
For in a distant hedgerow, there sits my plastic bag

A Hint of Grey

Who comes amidst this darkness, with eyes to pierce my soul
Moves softly through the moonlight, the clouds they seem to roll
What manner of beast before me, that it should seek me out
My heart can beat no faster, and no words have I to shout

With silence on all horizons, the tension starts to ease
I smile at my own failings, and then drawn to nearby trees
A look that talks of mischief, has now just caught my eye
A coldness grabs my very core, and my mind it starts to fly

Stepped from the painted mountains, to roam across the plains
Now stares in my direction, what cunning in these veins
Sat so close I see her breath, as she steps forth to greet
A descendant of the wolf itself, sits boldly near my feet

Her gaze is like no other, and slowly I am drawn
Content to sit and watch me, we share the coming dawn
The morning light reveals her, a coat as black as coal
I lie beside the fireside and slowly she does fall

And that was how it started, who knows how it will end
To walk beside me always, the stranger who became a friend
Who can show me loyalty and all that it can mean
It found me in the darkness and for the better I have been

The Straight and Narrow

In the shadow of this giant, with dust upon its brow
A fine pair stood in silence, the sun lifts on yonder knowe
And present my friend his harness, for he knows this rugged course
To follow in his footsteps, one man and his heavy horse

We step into a golden sun, what an entrance he does make
A muscled frame does saunter forth, as the land it does awake
This smell of horse and leather, as we slowly make our way
To roam the straight and narrow, upon this fine April day

And there upon the horizon, I see our trusty plough
It waits on our arrival, but we saunter even now
I clap my hands upon his flank, and the three of us unite
With reins held firm within my grasp, to venture forth till night

We roam the fields together, as man and horse do bond
As strong as he is relentless, of his nature I am fond
And when the day is over, and the sun does turn her back
I drift into a peaceful place, as we walk this well-known track

To think upon these days of old, oh the hardship they did face
Their stories long gone with them, and their names without a trace
Here's to them and their horse, who walked into a setting sun
Proud harness hangs upon the wall, for they worked the land as one

The Wanderers

How crisp this autumn morning, as their breath did fill the air
The morning dew did glisten and the mist had not a care
Yet they huddled amidst this backdrop, a rising sun to lift their mood
Set forth this group of shadows, who carried all they could

To peer into this wall of grey, for it to just stare back
They carried on regardless, only footsteps to mark their track
The morning haze was lifting, as the sun did settle a score
What perils lie before them, when just at that four more

What drives a soul to the unknown, and follow another man's lead
Trust those who went before them, for this is a calling indeed
I called unto these worthies, as the silence it was broken
To wave in my direction, yet not a word was spoken

The morning haze now vanquished, the sun did lift its veil
As I scan the far horizon, I knew they would not fail
To see figures in the distance, O that I should be so keen
With the sun upon their faces, amidst so many shades of green

Yet here they come triumphant, their goal is now in sight
So little that can halt them, as they give it all their might
But they curse the sound of thunder, and scowl at the morning snaw
It's a different kind of madness, those who chase the wee white baw

Breathless

The shades of red had left me, and the clouds had all turned tail
Blue sky embraced with darkness, when I heard the faintest wail
And we turned as one to face her, to this sound I'd heard before
Only fear stood there before us, for she walked in sight no more

And we stared upon the unknown, not sure I wanted to see
For there amidst the silence, this heartbeat belonged to me
That I should know such places, but such as they exist
Not for me in all the daylight, the twilight or the morning's mist

From the tower to the battlefield, to that lonely hanging tree
Sat perched on castle ramparts, to the sandbanks in the sea
That face at yonder window, the whispers in the upstairs room
Soft footsteps upon the concrete, to a feeling of certain doom

No thoughts of conversation, anxious looks from those who hear
Brave souls will talk of reason, for the one so very near
But some who felt that presence, or a fleeting glance there way
Are drawn by what awaits them, through the night or even day

Alas I shall not join them, but I hope they find their prize
To lie here with an open mind, until I see it with my own eyes
Whether you've seen or heard them, I always thought of them as dead
To lie warm beneath the blankets, and then it sat upon my bed

Unison

What thoughts lie in the darkness, what takes me to this place
The sights and smells before me, to make a young heart race
Carried upon the morning breeze, like leaves in an autumn stream
The sunshine brought her shadows, as I stepped amidst this dream

I gazed forth upon every horizon, that I should take this in
To remember all these faces, O the places they have been
As I stared upon the masses, for they walked forth row on row
Like the footsteps of the legion, in the distant sky a glow

And I stared upon this brightness, as it reached unto the sky
Voices rang out before me, and yet I knew not why
What of this dream before me, nothing like this in the past
For we sang like no tomorrow, not sure that I could last

I climbed the highest steps I'd seen, before me a field of green
These pipes and drums before me, the finest I had seen
And there we stood in unison, my very heart did soar
In the shadow of a lion rampant, and to a man we heard it roar

Skein

The cold air nipped my nostrils, my fingers clenched so tight
So peaceful at the water's edge, as I scan the coming light
With every sense on full alert, amidst the sleet and hail
My companion looks to the heavens, and I note her wagging tail

The morning sky is empty, but I know they are on the way
For our guest comes in darkness, but when I cannot say
I watch an ear lift gently, and then I hear it too
O the sound of geese in winter, whose number only grew

The north shore sees their entrance, just as the sun breaks through
To illuminate their dawn formation, every movement swift and true
Their calls can get no louder, when they bank as one to land
And they dance upon the water, like the sound of clapping hands

We gazed upon this marvel, in the hundreds three or four
Yet we moved at speed towards them, they were slowly joined by more
I felt my heartbeat quicken, as we reach the chosen spot
Our guests are none the wiser, and I picture a simmering pot

When just at that a stranger, should move and catch my eye
Grey wings so distinctive, and then we heard its cry
Their lift off left me speechless, in the hundreds three or four
But did tip my hat to the heron, and the taste of geese no more

In the Great Hall

The beast roared in defiance, for our number was now two
Just the grey mare sat beneath me, and her rider all but through
I called unto the darkness, my echo passed down the cave
My friends lay slain around me, time now my soul to save

A distant growl came nearer, so I turned my mare to bolt
She wailed and kicked her anger, and to freedom with a jolt
To hear the beast behind me, for its stride was a thunderous pace
I made for the cave's light entrance, as heart and mind did race

My thoughts did turn to living, and held on with all my might
When there upon the distance, a second beast did cross my light
We had never talked survival, our chances were but few
For every horse and rider present, not one did know of two

So we charged what stood before us, as my mare did start to wail
For its smell did fill her nostrils, but even now she did not fail
And in those final seconds, sword poised to strike its prize
A short rein and a last breath, and did see its very eyes

I lay broken and hardly breathing, as my mare gave out her last
The claws had laid her open, but I held her until she passed
I smelt its breath above me, as the beast's head lowered to me
And the voice did growl softly, "stop putting mushrooms in your tea"

A Single Chap

I recall my first encounter, I could not forget the stare
Some would say a natural, certainly a touch of flare
Amidst the words and groaning, I thought I heard a clap
I gazed across the table, and at that a single chap

Here's to the world of dominoes, and them that make it so
Behold the novice and the amateur, all hail the village pro
For they gathered every Thursday, in that familiar low lit room
And come the magic hour, silence and then eyes doon

Yet they came from all four corners, they had to get their fix
Whether league or county players, with the usual bag of tricks
There were players of all ages, bandits young and old
With one thing all in common, dominoes had its hold

Some would favour speech play, the thinkers sit and stare
Mind games at each table, like the tortoise and the hare
Where some will drum their fingers, others wear a constant frown
The smirk that says you're chapping, and then you lose your down

Whether amateur or professional, the A teams and the B's
The ones that tell the ghosters, the cheats and other C's
With tables and chairs now empty, and trophies to the usual mix
And ponder what just happened, and how I'm left holding double six

Passengers

What of this rag doll flying, where did the poor thing land
I felt the cold touch of reality, to my mouth did lift a hand
As all around me slowed down, I felt my mouth go dry
The silence of those beside me, did someone start to cry

Yet helpless has no colour, for I would paint it red
Like the road now laid before me, witness to her twitching dead
And they came like no tomorrow, but time itself stood still
To feel numb beside the blue light, for death had slipped her pill

The siren so very distant, had called my senses too
A mix of guilt and what if, here sit the chosen few
My gaze fixed upon the foreground, I knew where she did land
Her saviour stood there helpless, on the road her outstretched hand

And just like that we're moving, when all had ceased to move
The wheels of life start turning, we settle into a familiar groove
But temptation called me over, and I told myself don't stare
And beneath that flapping blanket, a glimpse of curled red hair

Loon

Nothing like it in the city, or even the nearest toon
To the village or the hamlet, to find yourself a loon
You will know it when you see it, for it's likely you will hear
The wisdom of a turnip, as nothing sits between each ear

This harmless kind of crater, when first I gave him sight
At first I thought eccentric, but I doubt he'd seen the light
The smile suggested friend not foe, his appearance suggested broke
To ponder all life had taught him, and that was when he spoke

He had travelled all four corners, and had sailed the seven seas
Crossed the Rockies and the Andes, he'd climbed the tallest trees
Stood bold before the grizzly charge, and felt the camel spit
In that bunnet and his wellies, with a rolled fag always lit

He'd known hardship and adversity, bad luck he had the lease
Fame and fortune were but strangers, but he savoured his jeely piece
To face his share of danger, a limp that made him sway
He had my every sympathy, although it changed leg every day

But his stories had me laughing, his humour I could endorse
He knew his ash from elder, but he could never pick a horse
When last I heard his whereabouts, the legend of the loon
Wellies striding towards the horizon, with his guiding light the moon

Ride On

And there I sat contented, amidst the April sun
New growth did fill the garden, the winter was almost done
I pondered what lay before me, to know where I should start
To find sanctuary in the old shed, not sure I had the heart

I gazed upon my neighbour's lot, it was perfection even now
How could grass look that good, I sat and scratched my brow
I primed the trusty lawnmower, it had never let me down
But it was stuck in hibernation, my complexion was like a clown

With defeat upon the horizon, several expletives I did howl
My attention was drawn elsewhere, as my neighbour's dog did growl
I tried a soothing word or two, but her heckles sat too high
Retreat was fast approaching, when a second dog caught my eye

It kind of looked half collie, to me some sort of cross
They bounced around the garden, for certain he was boss
I gazed around in wonder, the sight that now befell me
My shed gave me a front seat, his motion like a fiddler's elbie

Thereafter I sat in silence, in the presence of several mice
When just at that my neighbour, should appear with sound advice
"It'll be fine once it gets started", and suggested several tweaks
Aye things will look real different, given nine or ten more weeks

Salvation

At last I reach my summit, to stop and gulp the air
So many miles in each direction, when all you do is stare
Blue skies above and beyond me, and the snow a blinding white
To see my footsteps in the distance, a path that started at first light

I commit this sight to memory, and slip on my trusty pack
A loud crunch with every footstep, then see the snow ridge crack
Silence for one split second, this next bit is off the map
My focus turned to downhill, and then I felt the ankle tap

Dropped amidst a sea of white, and hurtling towards who knows what
In the company of half the mountainside, somewhere south a likely spot
I listen to my grunts and groans, so feeble amidst a building roar
Tumbled this way and the other, not sure I can take much more

Brilliant white is replaced by darkness, like a bed sheet pulled too high
My breath is pounded from me, as I give out a final sigh
All I know is downwards, no thoughts or words to say
So helpless I choose acceptance, to think of this my final day

So the roar decides to leave me, the plummet slows as I slip off
It all goes hushed and dreamlike, and at that I hear a cough
O that I should see this blue sky, when all was said and done
I feel the tears roll gently, and the glow of a winter sun

Sair

When first I knew his presence, I was prepared to let it go
If he would keep the noise down, for outside was deepest snow
But once he knew my habits, well then all hell broke loose
It was passed the point of talking, for I had myself a moose

His front room was my kitchen, he got three meals a day
Our taste in food was similar, no complaints did come my way
But certain habits caught my eye, he was prone to have a chew
His likes were cosmopolitan, for he favoured old and new

But his motions behind the cooker, or any corner space
Saw my investment in a spring trap, and did find his favourite place
Some will favour tattie, or even a wee bit of cheese
He'd dined at the finest table, so it was chocolate if you please

For sure he had a light touch, he'd played the game before
He cleared the plate of chocolate, and then came back for more
I was running out of options, my trap was never set so light
Not sure that he would notice, as I listened through the night

The trap had moved position, and then I saw the tail
His gaze was in the distance, how I wished that I had failed
The bloodied trap was lifted, ashamed to hold my prize
His ears and whiskers perfect, and then he blinked his eyes

To the Last

The roars had all but vanished, as they parted in the dark
Claws ripped upon their faces, none left without a mark
And in that morning daylight, scars of battle for all to see
The victor's mane resplendent, the defeated did turn and flee

Sunlight had brought a new day, and a changing of the guard
Some wounds can last a lifetime, more than skin is often scarred
The new king roars in defiance, as the open plain did hear
Young cubs were slain before them, as those who could draw near

What anguish for the defeated, the blood ran down his chin
Life would have new meaning, he had lost all kith and kin
He slowly licked his open wounds, torn flesh his only prize
To stare into the distance, birds above him circled high

Nothing moved within this furnace, all shimmered within that haze
With shade his only companion, what of the coming days
Head propped against the tree stump, he slowly drifted into sleep
Everything kept its distance, in time they would surely reap

But when the darkness lifted, alas he was not there
A wayward track showed his direction, towards that favourite lair
And as he passed his victor, that mane and frame so large
Blood dripped with every movement, just breath for one last charge

Lucky Dip

A stranger in a crowded room, just looking for some heat
The shot glass looked half empty, until I felt the taste of peat
A warm fire called me over, and I slowly made my way
I dropped into a soft chair, it had been one hell of a day

I should have smelled him coming, but I heard the primal grunts
The face looked worn and battered, some tumbles and well-aimed dunts
His red eyes looked me over, to the toilet with a look of disdain
But his hand-eye skills were lacking, his trousers bore the map of Spain

I nodded in his direction, as I didn't know what to make
For he stood there only staring, and I recall his subtle shake
He made his way to the barman, to emit a lowly growl
When his fist did hit the counter, I knew he was on the prowl

But they filled his glass in goodwill, and he slowly took a sip
And we sat almost expectant, holding tickets in a lucky dip
The bar did start to empty, had they seen this before
Alas the fire had won me over, I could stand a little more

And sure enough he came over, it turned out I was on his seat
His fist was primed for action, but then gravity had him beat
I could not catch the accent, I think I caught his name
For as I tried to lift him, the voice slurred "Leemie Alane"

This Way and That

I recognise the shadow, as I pass his favourite tree
His golden breast shines brightly, a cock pheasant looks down at me
A lofty perch for safety, followed by a daily routine
To roam the woods at leisure, his preference to go unseen

We've known him for several centuries, for the Normans let him go
There are many variations, but their pace is always slow
But it pays to be so wary, for the pheasant is quite a prize
From the gentry to the poacher, they would see to his demise

Yet it's the fox that causes havoc, to the cock pheasant and the hen
To leave a calling card of feathers, and mass murder in the pen
Their learning curve is rapid, as the pheasant knows his ground
To sit tight or run forever, a survivor pound for pound

You have to admire the pheasant, for all that comes his way
Well dressed and always strutting, what a call to end the day
And when the shooting is over, to find himself a mate
Where cockfights often prove fatal, it must be quite a date

For survival of the fittest, the cock pheasant fits that mould
Man and weather seldom beat him, his flight is high and bold
To evolve amidst such hardship, his story is surely proof
But no chapter yet on road sense, eyes closed and hear that doof!

The Nod

His eyes ran down the paper, I waited for them to stop
He glanced in my direction, and I knew that I was caught
But he smiled and slowly nodded, then his hand came to a halt
To whisper "Peeping Tom at 3:10," he was generous to a fault

But gems like this are rare finds, better heard from the horse's mouth
Beware any thing called a sure thing, for that's a bet going south
Many will follow a system, others will use a pin
Blank expressions and the headshakes, and for sure the fix was in

There is nothing like the horses, that's what I heard them say
Some will go for the straight win, others live and breathe each way
The real action is at the race track, the anticipation before the race
Roars and cheers on the home stretch, to know a loser by his face

I put my trust in fellow man, as the time approaches 3:10
Held tight my roll of twenties, my sweating hand on the bookies pen
My shaking hand gets the better of me, and my nerve sees me undone
To see him lead from start to finish, and romp home at 20-1

To have the courage of your conviction, O I know this loser's face
A gift from a total stranger, my lack of trust misplaced
So here's to taking chances, my homestretch I now plod
When I bump into that stranger, with a smile and a single nod

Allsorts

Alas the day of judgement, as all around stand still
Your wares laid out before you, to journey through that till
A time of calm reflection, will all of this suffice
Distracted by a smiling uniform, and then stunned by a total price

It started with my grand entrance, as the double doors did part
To get my own free basket, it felt like a brand-new start
I step onto the dance floor, and feel the blast of warming air
A casual glance from security, but for some it's the proper stare

With trolleys on the race track, it really is quite a sight
Near misses and head on collisions, yet everyone so very polite
Background music dulls the mind, as the two for ones make sense
I've got two at home already, but it's only pounds and pence

I don't know why I do it, but I'm drawn to what others buy
A quick glance whilst in the passing, to think is that worth a try
Spotting drinkers is a habit, with their bottles tucked out of sight
The grazers don't stop chewing, and shoplifters move like light

It really is quite relaxing, it even makes me smile
To switch off as you first walk in, and then drift from aisle to aisle
Few things in life are certain, go home and check that receipt
You don't get much for a tenner, I'll see you there next week

First Impression

Huddled close beneath the canopy, they listened but no-one spoke
Humid silence clung to the forest, content they sat and smoked
Nothing else seemed to matter, as their cloud did slowly lift
Primitive man could not appreciate, how far that smoke would drift

So when strangers came a-calling, to be inquisitive yet bold
The white man smelled its potential, their stained fingers holding gold
With all vessels fully laden, to set off with many a find
But little could they realise, there was nothing like its kind

0 what an introduction, to feel the initial hit
The smell and that sensation, its light touch when I am lit
And in that very instant, unaware of its lasting appeal
Its addictive qualities had me, yet to know what it would steal

How many have known this feeling, their number who can say
From the time of that encounter, to this its present day
What cost to all and sundry, such misery and pain
For something to look so innocuous, and how many has it slain

Yet it has travelled all four corners, accepted near and far
To mingle among all classes, but has always left a scar
But to be at that first encounter, in the centuries now far off
To those with their stained fingers, ya boy sir that's some cough

The Big Brown

I curse my foolish actions, and all that I have done
The bitter taste of complacency, to think that I had won
To hear his every footstep, I ponder what lies ahead
Claws grate into the door frame, and all I know is dread

With a cold sweat now upon me, I check the lock once more
For a shadow lurks on the outside, pressed hard against the door
His breath and grunts are menacing, his odour fills the air
To stare through the toughened windows, and there I meet his glare

Blue skies above the wilderness, no voice or soul to see
Isolation in its truest form, was how it's meant to be
Rivers run so deep and pure, the Redwoods reach so high
Air had never smelled so good, in this lifestyle I had to try

Such a landscape is unforgiving, in beauty lies the mask
A simple unseen error, and nature takes me to task
I plunder the pools of salmon, to catch what I did need
I clean the fish on the banking, and therein lies the deed

Paws thump hard against the door, I think we soon shall meet
All I know and hold dear, drowned out by my heartbeat
So I roar in pure defiance, there's no such thing as fate
Life changes in an instant, oh look here comes his mate

Dark

The curtains swept before me, the voice did say goodnight
I watched the door close gently, and with that goodbye all light
And in that very instant, with only silence by my side
This boy pulled up the covers, and from the darkness he did hide

The blackest kind of darkness, is the sort you find outside
Not the fir wood or the rock cave, just a thunderous windswept night
The moon will have no mention, as for stars there are no trace
To hear what moves beside you, but not the hand before your face

The coldest feel to darkness, is found within the deep
Such depths and lonely fathoms, where pressure knows no sleep
Light has never been there, a scene visited by the few
A resting place for victims, rusted vessels and their crew

The strangest part of darkness, is found in the ruins of old
Where murder danced with mayhem, cruel acts that went untold
To venture there in daylight, but that comfort will not last
For the screams that once did echo, still linger from the past

And then you meet true darkness, for that you must look within
It will not announce its presence, but it's there in her or him
To seldom stand before you, look for it if you dare
And as darkness looks upon you, meet the beast that left its lair

Recall

To lie dormant within each person, like postcards from a bygone time
The good and bad experiences, these memories yours and mine
So many you cannot count them, and yet they always last
For in a moment's notice, I return there to my past

Such moments are but fleeting, how often I cannot tell
But the sharpness of this detail, brought on by a sense of smell
To see what lies before me, as I reach out to touch
But what passes up my nostrils, appears to mean as much

Some I meet more often, like the smell of fresh cut grass
And see a man behind his mower, his life has long since passed
To journey upon public transport, bus fumes both inside and out
I almost see the school tie, to hear young voices shout

Chlorine so very distinctive, as I see the old swimming pool
Tiled floors that gleamed so brightly, as we travelled there from school
And that smell within the classroom, I find that hard to describe
To meet it in many a building, it's a smell that cannot hide

Perfume has its moments, I will not go into detail
But a gentle waft so sudden, sharp memories that never fail
The morning sees my favourite, I encounter it the most
Both young and old to savour, and its qualities I hereby toast

The Line

First light saw their coming, as they set out in line
Hushed voices moved in unison, for July month is their time
Such worthies are a rare bunch, from morning light till last
A way of life for centuries, the same footsteps in the past

The weather would not beat them, it was all that they could stand
To know what lay before them, for they were men of the land
To scan what stood so silent, to recognise the stray
And poise briefly at that imposter, how swiftly they would slay

The acres slowly rolled by, with the occasional backward glance
Amidst a sea of conformity, the mind could slip into trance
No time to be absent-minded, for one would come to check
Better seen the first time, to avoid that painful trek

So they grabbed a piece at lunchtime, and some they had a fag
But the pace was unrelenting, and seldom did they lag
With the heat of day upon them, their trusty spade in hand
The last acres done in silence, as they trudged that final stand

With nods of their approval, the sun slipped beneath a hill
What lay in wait tomorrow, as the countryside stood still
But that was in the future, for now a dram and a reel
For they burled like no tomorrow, those who walked the tattie dreel

Trespass

Footsteps upon the morning dew, of a stranger I have yet to meet
To see them on several occasions, and yet we have still to greet
Its presence had me puzzled, to wander upon the grass
To set up home on my patch, what some would call trespass

And yet I have no worry, for these footsteps are but small
But a presence to go unseen, and never hear his call
I don't believe in fairies, and it's not the neighbour's cat
For my rockery is its haven, where he often leaves his scat

I have sat and quietly waited, that our paths would finally cross
To be amicable where possible, at the same time I was boss
Such a meeting never happened, it truly had me beat
The cold night air was draining, and with that I did retreat

And then a strange thing happened, as my neighbour's dog did bark
I glimpsed between the curtains, as a nearby car did park
For there before the headlights, at last I got first sight
The halogen bulbs shone brightly, and to the bushes with all his might

I boldly marched towards him, and dropped unto my knees
The ball of spines came forward, and I counted all his fleas
I put forward several options, and suggested he could pick it
Alas he kept his own counsel, and was off to the village wicket

The Depth of It

With the sunshine all around me, I see my shadow reaching out
But the rest of me is frozen, and I am in no doubt
For just beyond that shadow, there sits my biggest fear
And yet it calls me over, and slowly I move near

This ragged edge before me, I know the depth in feet
But the comfort of that number, means nothing as we now meet
I feel the wind embrace me, the gusts and shrieks close by
To know that I must do this, but my feet are loathe to try

But I shuffle ever closer, my calf muscles start to shake
I kneel briefly for a moment, one small glimpse is all I'll take
A hawk rises from out of nowhere, and hovers as if to mock
To ride upon the thermals, then leave as I take stock

My pride is left behind me, upon my belly I now crawl
To clench this grass so tightly, with each breath I give it all
Reach out my hand before me, and on that edge do place
A shaking hand does follow, as heart and mind now race

All movement now by inches, the wind buffets around my head
A groan at what awaits me, and all I know is dread
To finally clear the cliff edge, this glimpse is so hard to take
I sensed that I stopped breathing, the deepest stare a man will make

Time Stood Still

To crave the open spaces, as they ventured across the land
Almost always fully laden, yet they often sit unmanned
Their pace is always steady, to cross each road or trail
For in haste there lies the danger, the pull of a sudden fish tail

They appear in all shapes and sizes, and their prices vary too
From modest to palatial, but they always have a loo
Some would curse their presence, not sure that I'm a fan
But once you make that purchase, your true love is a caravan

To often travel the roads alone, more often you meet a pair
The convoy that sits behind them, would drive a soul to despair
But to sit at a constant fifty, whether daytime or the night
With their wagon trail behind them, in darkness a column of light

Still they journey forth regardless, to gather there like a flock
On that hill or windswept coastline, to ponder all life and take stock
And here they sit contented, to admire all that can be seen
To make that same return journey, O the places they have been

Take your holidays when you can, and escape to that favourite place
Or buy yourself a caravan, and forget the human race
When just like that they vanish, the next sighting who can say
Few things in life are certain, until the next bank holiday

Hope

Where minutes have no meaning, and time just passed me by
I hold this hand so tightly, reassurance I can but try
All that once had mattered, no longer to cross my mind
Life's journey has new meaning, and all there is to find

What of the coming moment, when all I sense is fear
The feeling of uncertainty, for the one I hold so dear
But the time is almost upon us, to see it this very day
To be calm amidst the excitement, I even have time to pray

That I should feel so helpless, it surely must be close
Who knows what lies before us, but to know what matters most
My mind and heart are racing, so many voices I now hear
Hours of pain and anguish, when at that she just slips clear

To hear the cries of a newborn, the tears did fill my eyes
To smile and cry in unison, the gift of life to realise
Some did count her fingers, whilst I did count her toes
She had her mother's eyes, and she had her father's nose

No words to describe this feeling, as I gaze upon this sight
To the one so very fragile, we stared with all our might
And there we all sat contented, life would never be the same
Not a word was spoken, so many voices she did tame

Phantom

To circle like a buzzard, and see what passes by
Watching every subtle movement, some coast as others fly
But nothing goes unnoticed, as they venture from their lair
More often you see a single, though it's possible to see a pair

Always mindful of their quarry, to understand their cunning way
This search is unrelenting, to put the miles in every day
But their habits are unusual, to hunt in broad daylight
In full view of the intended, and never seen at night

Such tactics prove successful, as they come back for more
Like the lion upon the great plain, but I never heard this one roar
To never see their footprints, they don't howl at the fullest moon
I believe their pace is constant, to be upon you fairly soon

The weather does not deter them, to strike in dry or wet
Most victims will surrender, although on occasion tête-à-tête
And in that very moment, to know that you are caught
Nothing to do or say now, for such actions matter not

I prefer a constant awareness, assume they are always there
Lurking in the shadows, at times I sense their stare
But to relax for just that moment, they emerge from shadow or thicket
Few see this phantom coming, but their windscreen will see its ticket

Shadows

To hold this cup so tightly, the warmth spread through my grasp
The smell had won me over, both hands my soup did clasp
I peered upon a winter's day, blue sky and frost did meet
To those who sit beside them, and live life upon the street

For their gaze is often upwards, from their spot upon the ground
With damp in close attendance, and isolation all around
Cold air is a cruel companion, it prevents the deepest sleep
To be uncertain of your surroundings, in the dark of night to meet

What lies in wait for the homeless, a life lived day by day
The future has no meaning, and prospects who can say
A cup of soup is a godsend, a haven is a cardboard box
The kind act of a stranger, as they exist like the urban fox

How many have felt hypothermia, when wearing all your clothes
Damp clothes getting damper, hands and feet now froze
Winds that cut you to the bone, there is little you can do
The elements are unforgiving, yet their mindset "see it through"

To raise your hands to the fire, feel hot water upon your skin
Warm beneath the bed sheets, safe in the home you live in
So spare a thought for the homeless, the next time that you pass
And when frost lies among the shadows, think how long would you last

Lost

Here they stand in unison, a never ending sea of green
I approach the timeless forest, her nature that goes unseen
Slip past the gate to sanctuary, at once I feel her peace
All troubles now left behind me, and there I fell at ease

A gust blows through the tree tops, and with it a gentle lean
The rustle of leaves is soothing, to hear it and know the serene
Amidst the hard and soft woods, some planted as others grow wild
Fire breaks invite the sunlight, the wind whistles like a child

She changes with every season, her moods change through the day
Her residents have grown accustomed, their number who can say
The trails like modern highways, a nibble here and there
To exist among the shadows, on occasion to meet their stare

And then I see the tree stumps, what of this open sore
Just the silence of desolation, as nothing stands here any more
At last I find a witness, a silver birch standing guard
Stood quiet beside the wood pile, and a landscape badly scarred

Yet new growth reaches upward, whether wild or by design
My footsteps getting slower, as I near the final climb
With body and soul replenished, and time the only cost
My feet never leave the footpath, how good to feel this lost

Above and Beyond

Stood tall amidst the silence, not much for them to say
To gaze upon human nature, in night and through the day
Their number has slowly risen, for this is a worthy cause
How often they go unnoticed, until now when I do pause

From the streets within our cities, to that rural village green
A protector of every age group, how many can be this keen
They always put a shift in, and seldom are they beat
It is an altruistic effort, that each of us shall meet

I know the chill of winter, the darkness and bitter cold
It's a thought to venture outdoors, yet here they remain so bold
Almost an act of defiance, for there they stand alone
What it must take to endure, like an athlete in their zone

To stand above all others, they have a certain glare
I would not say superior, but I almost sense a stare
To find them on the corner, or on the steepest hill
Upon the straight and narrow, and our countryside so still

And there upon the horizon, in numbers it's quite a sight
To be homeward bound in safety, in the glow of our streetlight
Yet only now I realise, they have lit our way and how
Lined out into the distance, then I see their gentle bow

Here and There

This tiger walks behind me, so close I dare not glance
His reflection in a window, a look that was pure chance
To know my every movement, he can even match my pace
I try to hear him breathing, as my beating heart does race

Can you smell that tiger, I sometimes think it's true
Is that his pungent aroma, but no paw prints on the dew
I wonder where he came from, I must have crossed his trail
To find solace in the library, the receptionist said "rogue male"

Did you hear the tiger, alas I didn't hear a thing
But the silence spoke of something, and its presence crowded in
Both heart and pulse bore witness, my mouth completely dry
A sense of true foreboding, yet a part of me asked why

Have you touched the tiger, yes I almost grabbed his tail
But self-preservation kicked in, and a part of me did fail
I should have turned to face it, but they always say don't stare
For its presence was a comfort, and the rest of me did care

So long my faithful tiger, who did not have a name
What to call a wild thing, that I would never tame
Here's to modern medication, that's what the doctor said
I miss my friend the tiger, but still check beneath my bed

Something In the Air

I felt the midge upon me, I'd known him since a child
To do my share of scratching, in the high places and the wild
But here upon the river, that I should be chest deep
He'd brought his family with him, a routine they liked to keep

It's hard to ignore their presence, as they dance around your ears
To land upon my bare skin, and reduce their host to tears
The humid air had roused them, they would need an evening meal
I cursed them in their hundreds, and lay down my rod and reel

So I sat in complete acceptance, there is nothing quite so thrawn
As my humble friend the midgee, when just like that he's gone
And I turned at once in wonder, expecting to see their cloud
A darker presence loomed above me, its blackness like a shroud

Should I wade to the banking, but that rumble held me back
The tree lined shore was waiting, and then I heard the crack
The island was my haven, as I lay silent in the night
So many shades of blackness, then a sudden flash of light

To see it from a distance, I always thought a wondrous sight
But as I lay beneath its fury, I truly felt its might
The crashing sound slowly drifted, the light no more to see
How thankful amidst the darkness, and the touch of that midgee

Edge

Goodbye to this sweet horizon, amidst a towering wall of grey
We drop into its very depths, who dare to come this way
A howling wind calls upon us, it swirls about the deck
Her shrieks call out a warning, but we keep our fear in check

For somewhere in this maelstrom are souls upon life's edge
Our light will dissolve their darkness, as we redeem this pledge
What of this task before us, and the path that lies ahead
With seas beyond all measure, to put others first instead

Life tossed in all directions, at the mercy of something vast
A good time for a prayer, for into peril they are cast
All others have taken shelter, they truly are life's last hope
Crashing waves show no mercy, this courage bonded like a rope

All eyes upon the darkness, the wind and spray to meet
A faint light on the horizon, this single flare does greet
But the night is far from over, as mother nature does unleash
To be held within such torment, unsure of her release

The morning light almost upon us, when finally she let us go
Their eyes awash with terror, a look that few will know
Their journey home so quiet, they had stared death in the eye
What of this edge before us, and the lifeboat crews who try

Still Here

It waits for me in darkness, to almost sense the fading light
This presence is a constant, within the quiet of every night
For in that calming silence, where breath and pulse remain
This unwanted invitation, and therein starts the game

To close my eyes on streetlight, distant noise just passes by
No thought within this moment, a little sleep is all I'll try
As all around will drift off, where time does not exist
I am held within this limbo, for insomnia will seldom miss

Relaxed within my stillness, how I dwell upon the dark
This mind without an off switch, lack of sleep to leave its mark
Distant trains that come and go, as planes pass overhead
Each noise is so distinctive, to curse them from my bed

So here I lie in expectation, in the hope that I drop off
This light changes every hour, as time alone does scoff
To stare upon that nearby clock, for it to just stare back
Whatever makes a good night's sleep, to know I've lost the knack

Car headlights upon the horizon, the early shift on their way
Sleep lies within my very grasp, step forth a brand-new day
The sunlight framed my curtains, as body and soul did slowly lift
If I could have just one wish, deep sleep that I might drift

Point of Origin

What of this light before me, but each of us did know
Such a scale is overwhelming, our horizon a golden glow
To admire it from a distance, as it raged into the sky
Flames danced upon dark canvas, a rugged landscape left to cry

We stepped into its very path, and I felt its warm embrace
She flitted through the treetops, with each burst it gathered pace
As we turned to change direction, this cruel wind did the same
Hand in hand they roared upon us, there was nothing here to tame

To know when you are beaten, I was empty to the core
Surrounded by this inferno, as life did close its door
Perched within this furnace, where all was set ablaze
Its deafening roar consumed me, to be lost within this haze

Yet at that very moment, each breath your last to take
I felt an inner calling, and every effort I should make
So I crawled into a dark place, not that I accept defeat
Hope cradled there beside me, the nearest thing to my retreat

To curse the flames about me, my hands would never be the same
For hell had washed upon me, and I heard it call my name
So tucked upon the high ridge, that would never look so green
If I should wake tomorrow, I know what life can mean

Speck

The snow had brought its silence with an all familiar cloak
Nothing moved upon the landscape, only plumes of fireside smoke
The mountain ash once laden, wears a coat of finest white
I scan what lies before me, when at that I catch first sight

To see it then to lose it, but to know that it is there
My hand to shield the sunlight, and a touch of winter glare
In the midst of my frustration, a glimpse of something small
Who roams beneath these white clouds, and then I hear its call

To soar upon the morning breeze, that I should have your view
Pushing higher with every moment, to be lost in all that blue
How far have you travelled, who even knows you are there
To peer down upon creation, as I look up to stare

I recognise your movement, I even know your name
Your reputation precedes you, I also know your game
I watch you slowly circle, as you pass overhead
Something has your attention, how long since you have fed

Dropped from sight in seconds, it almost took my breath
I lost sight behind the tall trees, who knows if life or death
White clouds against the blue sky, the cool breeze overhead
To vanish in an instant, but it left a splash of red

A Changing Landscape

Stood proud upon the river bank, its leaves are brushed with gold
To tower upon its brethren, and who can say how old
I have sat beneath its canopy, I watched the river go by
It changed with every season, in its shadow I would often lie

The strongest winds would call them, this giant would gently sway
Where others fell in surrender, it stood defiant come what may
An early spate to cleanse all, the river's force is quite a sight
But as that flood abated, to stand with all his might

I gazed upon a moonlit night, its silhouette was profound
For in that very moment, my breath the only sound
The stars were at their brightest, when I heard the loudest slap
I looked upon the ripples, as a stranger lay on his back

Many a guest will come and go, this one is here to stay
His habits are nocturnal, and he always has his say
I came to know his habits, I had seen the occasional sign
And when he started nibbling, I knew where he did dine

Farewell my poor leviathan, that you should be laid to rest
But the teeth marks were relentless, in the nightshift of this pest
A mighty crack a gentle sway, but this culprit did not leg it
Witness to the loudest crash, almost proud that he had felled it

The White Stuff

The blue frame made of plastic, its construction we could trust
And once you sat upon it, their pushing gave it thrust
But place it on a downslope, and cover that slope in snow
This child became a test pilot, with only one place to go

Conditions were picture perfect, with blue sky overhead
Final moments upon the hilltop, not much that needed said
And just like that I am moving, upon the firm glistening snow
Scarf wrapped below my armpits, there's nothing this pilot doesn't know

The shouts upon the distance, I watched the trees go by
Sat low in a tuck position, when all you do is fly
I had left the others trailing, they gave me plenty room
I may have hit the sound barrier, although I don't recall the boom

And in those final moments, the top speed left me cold
Where others had baled before me, I told myself be bold
Yet at that very moment, from the ground a column of steam
I jump before the collision, and with that I lose the dream

I gaze up toward the blue sky, my every inch covered in snow
Dazed by my sudden departure, I see my empty sledge still go
But I did not see the culprit, or what left its calling card
Just the reflexes of this pilot, and the prints of a St Bernard

Ubiquitous

And here they sit before me, their movement a gentle sway
I am held within their silence, for I seldom gaze this way
I wonder upon their number, as they stretch toward the sea
To roll into the unknown, the epitome of carefree

I stare upon the legions, not one of them in line
Did a part of me stop breathing, when a part of me called time
For in that very moment, I had left all things behind
I blink before the bright sky, and savour what I did find

Soft edges tipped with sunlight, their mass a changing grey
Bold swirls of white resplendent, newest blue gets in the way
Behold the darkest menace, who lingers at the rear
That it should carry mischief, as thunder growls in every ear

I see a giant laid out before me, a chariot without its horse
Others that look straight at me, a haunted face without remorse
Who else had looked upon them, as they disperse before my eyes
Like an ever-changing artwork, that will never be realised

The sun dropped below its horizon, all legions now laid to rest
Moonlight will see the stragglers, only one does wear a crest
The night will wear its darkness, nature's palette for all to see
For a canvas without rival, it sits above both you and me

Blinkered

Who knows the price of freedom, what value has free speech
Who makes that final decision, oh how they like to preach
Some have no voice or platform, so imagine if you will
That nature spoke in English, her stories would send a chill

Those from the coldest climates, whose fur dictates a price
Cruel snares that lie in waiting, flesh torn within its vice
To be held in that position, as pain and death close in
Howls of abject suffering, can you hear that hellish din

Those in the open ocean, who thrive throughout the seas
The myriad of detritus, their ecosystem on its knees
How many kinds of plastic, to float a thousand years
Their number will diminish, with no remorse or tears

The bear within its winter den, two cubs that suckle in
She gazes upon their every move, pressed close the warmest skin
Their quarry lies upon the ice, but that will soon be lost
When ice turns to open sea, we know what that will cost

Now gaze upon the smallest hands, this baby at her mother's breast
Safe and warm is all she asks, but life will still be a test
From the smallest to the largest, they all deserve a chance
That we should thrive together, and as one we all advance

Embrace

Where now the hunter gatherer, the distance they have come
That primitive way of living, such ways are surely done
For today we embrace technology, and all that it can be
The possibilities are endless, its effect for all to see

This constant communication, no matter where you are
Nothing here is sacred, at the table or in the car
Eyes glued upon a bright screen, as we witness the death of craic
No idle chat or banter, their fingers in a constant tap

Where everything is portable, to follow you to the grave
Lurking in that pocket, a way of life some crave
All manner of details made public, assume people want to know
To get their fix at first light, and so the day will go

Where information is solid gold, your data commands a fee
Your preference and your spending, there for all to see
Nothing here goes unnoticed, it shapes what lies ahead
Almost a sense of foreboding, the high street almost dead

Where then the hunter gatherer, it all comes down to cost
To understand what matters, to see what we have lost
We couldn't stop it if we wanted, its momentum has such pace
Here's to the next invention, for there goes the human race

H

Hidden within the hedgerow, some would say stealth mode
I shouted something different, as it stepped into the road
With heart and mind now racing, I stopped but I did stare
Sitting nonchalant before the vehicle, to be in the presence of a hare

To look in my direction, and then gaze left and right
Black tipped ears were twitching, what else lurked out of sight
It looked immaculate in the daylight, no fur was out of place
The amber eyes were striking, as it left without a trace

Days and weeks had passed by, when again our paths did meet
Lying quiet upon the grass field, with a young one at her feet
I would name him Hartley, and all his kith and kin
I recalled our first encounter, to think what might have been

The summer sun upon us, when all are laid at rest
They see what comes before them, the dark night a different test
I leave them in the sunshine, the field and hedge their home
Some of nature is watching, talons gripped upon a throne

This autumn chill upon me, stubble fields now turned to black
I see a gaze familiar, which Hartley is staring back
So bold upon the ploughed earth, his way of life to save
We stare upon each other, and I almost want to wave

Journey

To be huddled in their shelter, rain pelted all around
Here they stood and waited, when at last a familiar sound
It slowly rolled towards them, behold the open door
This haven of public transport, and forward they did pour

With favoured seats now taken, how slowly they made off
Nods and smiles between them, when all who could did cough
For this their daily journey, six miles there and surely back
To ponder what lay before them, thoughts drift upon this track

Some gazed through a window, or at a stranger's feet
The ones who talked forever, every secret from the street
Others would sit in silence, to hear the engine strain
To know the corners and that pothole, the condies and sunken drain

I looked upon their faces, then I saw an empty seat
To think when I last saw her, and the smile as we did meet
Her daughter sat beside her, the likeness for all to see
They came and went together, to think where they might be

Nobody appeared to notice, I never heard them say
Faces that would come and go, that seemed to be the way
Then one morning came the answer, for all of us did see
As she held that precious bundle, and their number now was three

Timeless

Fallen trees lie before me, here they lie to rot
Criss cross in one direction, the wind cares not a jot
The heather keeps them company, deepest moss beneath my feet
Where woodcock leap before me, so good that we should meet

The deer path runs beside them, to meander through the wood
I slowly walked upon it, the stillness of its mood
The wrens that dart before me, for them a fleeting glance
Most of nature does elude me, as it cannot take the chance

A single crow called its warning, to know I had been seen
My presence no longer a secret, that he should be so keen
Sunlight flickers through the branches, its warmth upon my face
To gaze in all directions, nothing moves within this place

I sat still within the silence, and listened for every sound
For some are sat around me, whilst others have gone to ground
This smell of pine does linger, and I slowly closed my eyes
The gentle breeze now blowing, and I start to realise

Time here has no bearing, light comes and goes each day
The same as the inhabitants, as they go on their way
The sunset calls me homeward, all of nature now left behind
To know that I will soon return, for there is so much here to find

Who Gave Their All

His gaze towards the horizon, to embrace the rising sun
A rifle upon his shoulder, his fighting days now done
For this a fitting memorial of those who fought and fell
The bloodied ground bore witness, for men who traversed hell

I see images of their hardship, with smiles they gather round
What lay in wait tomorrow, such pictures are profound
No words to explain this frontline, their eyes could only stare
Death stalks them from a distance, yet forward they would dare

Their hopes and all ambition, that other life is now on hold
The memories of love and laughter, is dulled by war's harsh mould
Treasured photos of their dearest, cherished images get them by
A heartfelt letter read repeatedly, may lead a man to cry

Amidst the din of shellfire, to dwell on those they've lost
The smiling faces and distant voices, to know what this has cost
Anxious looks within the ranks now, the barrage is about to stop
Hear the blast of a sergeant's whistle, and off they go up top

This sunset in the distance, the memorial's shadow starts to fall
Like so many of his brethren, they answered their countries' call
Survivors brought home their memories, their proud flag upon the sky
How precious the fallen's sacrifice, and why he now stands so high

Horizon

Sat within those four walls, a place they know as home
The good times and fond memories, the joy that all had known
To change within an instant, when choice is no choice at all
To leave it all behind you, must be life's hardest call

Just the clothes they were wearing, perhaps the smallest pack
All else was left behind them, and tears as they look back
To start a journey like no other, to hold their youngest's hand
What lies in store tomorrow, or where they even land

They walk until the darkness, and then they walked some more
Cold and hunger close companions, they would feel it to the core
Hope was all they had now, yet bravely they press on
To arrive upon the coastline, rolling waves to greet the dawn

To gaze upon the distant lights, for there salvation lay
Determined to the very last, it looked a short sail away
To depart amidst the darkness, their destination so very near
Families huddled close together, with all that they held dear

Waves that showed no mercy, they soon realise their plight
The west wind was unrelenting, and tipped them before first light
Screams lost within the darkness, bodies lay scattered upon the sand
What of their hopes and memories, and the smallest empty hand

Behold

Sat still within this silence, just the sound of my own breath
The coldness of her small hand, that sudden chill of death
To look so quiet and tranquil, she could almost be asleep
But today I lost my best friend, my heart and soul to weep

Her eyes have lost that sparkle, and the smile that meant so much
Her look that told me everything, the softness of her touch
My life took on new meaning, when she first walked by my side
I held her hand so firmly, I knew this was my bride

Her laughter in the distance, gentle ways that made me smile
She understood my every thought, my rough edges she did file
At night to hold her closely, and tell her how much she meant
This warm and caring body, to know she was heaven-sent

O that I should lose my best friend, this whole morning feels surreal
Our hopes and all ambitions, how quickly death does steal
One last whisper I love you, how gentle my final kiss
For all we shared together, and the love that I shall miss

Cherish

To hold me like no other, this was the lightest touch
My finger held so softly, in weeks to grow so much
Blue eyes that held me captive, no words had you to say
I held your hand so closely, for you made my every day

To hold my hand so firmly, for this first day of school
I think I was more nervous, you gave me the occasional pull
When at that gate I let you go, as a tear rolled down my cheek
And just before you went inside, I glanced your anxious keek

Those days so very precious, as I watch you slowly grow
To have your mother's intellect, she may have let me know
The child became a young lady, and let go her father's hand
To know it would always be there, wherever she might land

So many birthdays passed now, dark hair has turned to grey
Not much that I can tell you, for you will have your say
Choices made for good or bad, but still they must be made
I seldom see your familiar smile, but I know it will never fade

Time has turned full circle, as you walk yours to school
Little things that mean so much, with your life so very full
To lie here and think upon this, not much that I let slip
And as she now stands beside me, I feel her loving grip

One

The footsteps on this journey, how many until it is done
The sunrise and the darkness, when all of us are one
To understand its silence, for in that quiet I rejoice
Just the breath of all humanity, often better without its voice

Creed and colour was nothing, for we embraced them all
To see their smiling faces, on each of them we call
This journey that lies before us, that everyone shall take
The torment and the hardship, that we should see its wake

To understand its nature, to be locked within its grasp
All that is thrown upon you, to know it will not last
Pure bliss to shine so brightly, sorrow that hits you hard
Where love will hold you tightly, and fate will turn its card

Step forth within this maelstrom, what have we to lose
Naked at that first breath, love those that lit the fuse
Still we revel in our moment, all of this so very brief
The gift of life for the taking, where the smallest part is grief

The sunlight asked me over, its glory shone on me
Together we enjoy each moment, the best of it is free
I laughed and they laugh with me, and together we will stand
It all starts again tomorrow, who knows where it will land

In Appreciation of Ewe

Stood bold upon the hillside, half wild in their full dress
"The finest in the county", the old collie less impressed
And so the journey started, with their passengers looking on
Carlisle their destination, a wee hurl upon the dawn

To make a shilling at market, these rascals played the game
So many bonnets in close attendance, but who would take them hame
They raced into the sales ring, under many an inquisitive eye
Seconds that make the difference, the auctioneer's rapid cry

Their flicks and nods abundant, few will see it all
The gavel to slowly hover, but everyone heard it fall
Buys and tales were loaded, did someone have a dram
Their bonnets in the distance, the sales ring a perfect calm

And so the journey homeward, renewed friendship and that tiff
Packed out to the gunnels, and that all familiar whiff
The collie did slowly awaken, the tailgate hit the deck
Some leapt and others bolted, gate closed to end this trek

But their journey will continue, they have travelled 10,000 year
Endured hardship like no other, that wee bit grass so near
Their tale one of survival, and much to our relief
Stood bold upon the hillside, could almost be clan chief

Just the Two of Us

His entrance was electric, as he danced across the floor
To scurry up the skirting, but he didn't use the door
To disappear like magic, it could have been a dream
Touch down the ladies' cloakroom, even now I hear the scream

I was summoned in an instant, that I should know my fate
Fingers pointed in its direction, this beast that lay in wait
I closed the door behind me, the darkness concealing all
The torch was shaking gently, just my shadow upon the wall

Footsteps upon the tiled floor, it could hear my every move
To illuminate the nooks and crannies, in a swiftly sweeping groove
Did I say I'm scared of spiders, did I forget to say
This challenge with its eight legs, to meet this very day

The floor was slowly quartered, over there his resting place
But the rascal was a climber, and now we turn to face
That I should be so frozen, no thoughts or words do pass
It darted from the light beam, perhaps it saw the glass

Its descent was most alarming, to slip inside a leather bag
Mind and heart were racing, for now I had to blag
So I quickly flushed the toilet, such relief and their thank yous
If he should hit the dance floor, aye they often travel in twos

Dunking

Its origins are uncertain, when early man did risk it
Such mastery and technique, skills required to dunk a biscuit
No evidence upon cave paintings, early writings draw a blank
The name and date a mystery, to whom we have to thank

The Pharaohs built their pyramids, the Romans a well-built road
The Aztecs were canny builders, the Vikings brought their horde
But when the working day was over, how many reached for a brew
Their dry lips towards that chalice, did a biscuit come into view

Perhaps the early impressionists, empty canvas and their muse
When bereft of inspiration, grabbed a teabag to infuse
I think now I can see it, the masterpiece almost done
The final stroke is halted, artist and biscuit become one

That only leaves one question, their favourite on the day
Alas I know the answer, common sense to have its say
Behold the common digestive, for its history I can trace
But one second on the long side, a splash known to the human race

The Jaffa cake and Hobnob, a choice that many will know
Thinner versions like a Rich Tea, only handled by a pro
To be dunked for only seconds, amidst the brew and rising steam
But in search of true perfection, reach for that custard cream

The Awakening

Oh the peace of total quiet, my breath the faintest sound
To fall into such silence, this magic I have found
What brings me to this moment, the path that led to here
Few thoughts or feelings present, a sense of bliss so near

Something else does linger, to know I do belong
No fear of my surroundings, is that a distant song
Held in total comfort, to feel so much at ease
A dream unlike all others, subtle warmth like summer breeze

A sudden sense of movement, does someone come my way
But nothing spoils this moment, so relaxed I want to stay
So certain of a presence, is that a hint of light
The softness of this moment, I surrender to my plight

I feel this presence come closer, I thought I heard my name
Who knows where I am headed, I wish I could remain
To blink my eyes in wonder, bright lights do slowly hail
Her angelic voice was calling, that sofa's not in the sale

The Cheek of It

We gazed upon the burling cowl, our measurements almost done
This nagging doubt upon me, beneath a winter sun
The December chill was biting, and all had gathered round
Our consensus was for action, a solution must be found

Would he fit the chimney, to us it was a farce
His tunic would be manky, when filled with Santa's arse
So we checked our calibration, but it wasn't looking good
To hold his sack so tightly, and deliver in the nude

We considered all the options, and then we kicked the can
Someone said conspiracy, but I was not a fan
We would write to his good lady, that we were trying to help
We were looking for approval, and to avoid a festive skelp

With the first snowfall of winter, we put it in a letter
The text and tone were vital, did we no send a belter
All hope lay with the postie, the clincher tucked inside
The Christmas lights were gleaming, and every smile was wide

To wake that Christmas morning, the garden a sea of white
The letter worked its magic, presents bathed in morning light
But nothing came down the chimney, the problems we did foresee
As someone searched their handbag, farewell that front door key

A Change of Tack

To bite me in the morning, and try the same at night
To kick the stable loudly, flared nostrils left and right
Fourteen hands to the withers, taught muscle packed on bone
High spirited I would say so, there stood the meanest roan

A rascal from the outset, I'd known her since a foal
To stand out from the others, too much heart and soul
The farmer paid a fortune, she always caught the eye
Standing on her hind legs, hooves dancing in the sky

I admired her from a distance, she truly had it all
But complacent for a moment, full charge from nearby stall
It was my lack of bottle, the farmer said with glee
To sense my fear and caution, let's just wait and see

Weeks and months did pass by, but nothing came to pass
With every trick worth trying, she still tore upon the grass
The grips and bites reminders, to know she was the boss
But one solid kick too many, some lines you do not cross

If she was playing dirty, then clearly so would I
And just like that it ended, even now I hear his sigh
The farmer had the answer, of that there was no doubt
But it hadn't taken courage, only bottles of finest stout

Time Machine

To be made of finest walnut, and engraved with floral leaf
First sighted when aged seven, with a stir of disbelief
To hover above the sideboard, as I could only stare
Its legs were tucked beneath it, to be sitting in mid-air

To almost call me over, I tiptoed across the room
I picked it up and held it, O to hear that bonny tune
All who could came running, for this had pride of place
Touch down upon the sideboard, with a frown upon each face

And yet at every visit, to always turn and glance
To wonder where it came from, and waited for my chance
No mark or dust upon it, to me one of a kind
When lifted that very instant, and slowly she did wind

The visitors all turned quiet, this soft tune upon each ear
We shared a smile together, for her music box so dear
So when the music ended, to rest beside the fire
Yet it still played within me, from a tune I could not tire

How many tunes have played since, how many years have passed
Fond memories I am left with, where other things don't last
To now sit upon my sideboard, it still has pride of place
And when I slowly lift off, I can see each smiling face

A Final Note

I would like to thank my mother and my former work colleagues, Maureen Phillips and Lorna Edwards, for their words of encouragement to continue with my poetry and have it published in a book.

Donald Cameron